REFUSE, MISUSE, and Reuse

By Melanie Ostopowich

Raintree

Chicago, Illinois

Customer service: 888-363-4266
Visit our website at www.raintreelibrary.com
Published by Raintree, a division of Reed Elsevier, Inc.

Library of Congress Cataloging-in-Publication Data
Ostopowich, Melanie.
  Waste : refuse, misuse, and reuse / Melanie Ostopowich.
     p. cm. -- (Science at work)
Includes index.
Summary: Introduces the problem of garbage and the ways in which it may be disposed of or recycled.
  ISBN 0-7398-6996-5 (library binding-hardcover)
  1. Refuse and refuse disposal--Juvenile literature. 2. Recycling (Waste, etc.)--Juvenile literature. [1. Refuse and refuse disposal. 2. Recycling (Waste, etc.)] I. Title. II. Series: Science at work (Chicago, Ill.)
  TD792.O88 2004
  628.4--dc22
                                   2003007266
Printed and bound in the United States of America
1 2 3 4 5 6 7 8 9 0   07 06 05 04 03

About the consultant:
Ezra Glenn is a city planner who works for the City of Somerville, Mass., as director of economic development. He has extensive experience in environmental policy and natural resource protection.

Project Coordinator: Janice L. Redlin
Series Editors: Jennifer Nault, Jennifer Mattson
Consultant: Ezra Glenn
Design and Illustration: Warren Clark
Copy Editor: Tina Schwartzenberger
Layout: Bryan Pezzi
Photo Researchers: Tracey Carruthers, Wendy Cosh

Note to the Reader
Some words are shown in bold, **like this**. You can find out what they mean by looking in the glossary.

Photograph Credits
Every reasonable effort has been made to trace ownership and to obtain permission to reprint copyright material. The publishers would be pleased to have any errors or omissions brought to their attention so that they may be corrected in subsequent printings.

Cover: Bottles (**Digital Vision**), Boy with recycle bin (**PhotoSpin, Inc.**), Landfill (**Digital Vision**); **Corbis Corporation**: pages 3BL, 4TL, 20T, 20B, 36B; **Corel Corporation**: page 9B; **Digital Vision**: pages 2/3BKG, 3BR, 9T, 16T, 16B, 27, 35BL, 35BR, 38, 45R, 44-48BKG; **EyeWire, Inc.**: page 13TL; **Heather C. Hudak**: page 22T; **Istock.com**: pages 22B, 31, 32TR, 41, 43R, 45M; **Bryan Pezzi**: pages 7, 28; **PhotoAgora**: pages 23, 39R (Gary Mackey); **PhotoDisc, Inc.**: pages: 32TL, 37; **Photos.com**: pages 3T, 5TL, 5TR, 5BL, 6B, 8T, 11, 13TR, 15, 21, 24, 26, 30T, 30B, 32B, 33T, 34T, 35T, 36L, 36M, 36T, 39L, 40, 42L, 42R, 43L, 44, 45L; **Photovault.com**: pages 4TR, 4B, 5BR, 8B, 10, 29L, 36R; **Tom Stack & Associates**: pages 6T, 14, 18 (Thomas Kitchin), 17 (Doug Sokell); **Stock.xchg**: pages 25, 29R, 33B; **Visuals Unlimited**: pages 12 (Inga Spence), 13B (John Sohlden), 34B (Wally Eberhart).

Contents

Have you ever

wondered where your garbage goes when you throw it out,

or what garbage does to the environment,

or how your trash can be recycled?

Everyone knows about waste. We have all thrown garbage away or dropped something off to be recycled. We have all probably used something that was made from recycled materials.

Societies produce large amounts of waste every year. For example, 106 billion disposable pens are thrown away every year in the United States. The number of toothbrushes thrown away every year in New York City is almost equal to the weight of 240 medium-sized automobiles. This waste can be reduced by recycling items such as paper, glass, and plastic.

FINDING LINKS

Society

Everyone makes waste. Food, paper, plastic, and anything else you throw away is considered waste. The average American throws away 32 pounds (12 kg) of garbage a week. That adds up to 1,664 pounds (621 kg) of garbage a year.

The Environment

The amount of waste in the world has a big impact on the **environment**. There is only so much space in the world where we can put our waste. If waste is not handled properly, it could pollute the air we breathe, the water we drink, and the land on which we live.

Technology

Scientists have had to come up with creative ways to handle the waste produced in the world. From designing better **landfills** to developing new methods of recycling, scientists work to control the problem of too much garbage.

Careers

Many people work in the waste industry. For example, people pick up garbage from your house,  engineers design landfills, and scientists try to find better ways to recycle used objects. All of these people work to make Earth a cleaner place to live.

Refuse

"Will someone
take out
the trash?"

Refuse is another word for waste or garbage. It is the material you throw into the trash after you decide you do not need it anymore. People create garbage everywhere: in homes, businesses, schools, and hospitals.

Garbage is a reality of daily life. According to the latest estimates, 75 percent of all garbage sent to landfills can be recycled into other products. Many people are working hard to find new ways to recycle this material.

Who wants to talk about garbage?

How would you describe garbage? Does it look and smell disgusting? Is it something you want to throw in the trash can and forget about? Or do you see it as something that can be turned into something else and be used over and over again?

Only a small portion of the garbage you throw away is smelly and unappealing. Food waste, made up of rotting meat, fruits, and vegetables, is what makes our garbage smell bad. Only 8.9 percent of garbage is food waste. The remaining garbage includes plastic, glass, paper, and yard waste.

Much of the glass, paper, and plastic can be recycled.

Once we realize that not all garbage is disgusting, we can see it contains useful material. It is fascinating to learn how much of the garbage we throw away every day can be reused and recycled into new things.

> The average American creates about 4.5 pounds (2 kg) of trash each day. This is higher than the average 2.7 pounds (1.2 kg) produced each day in 1960.
>
> **BYTE-SIZED FACT**

What is in your garbage?

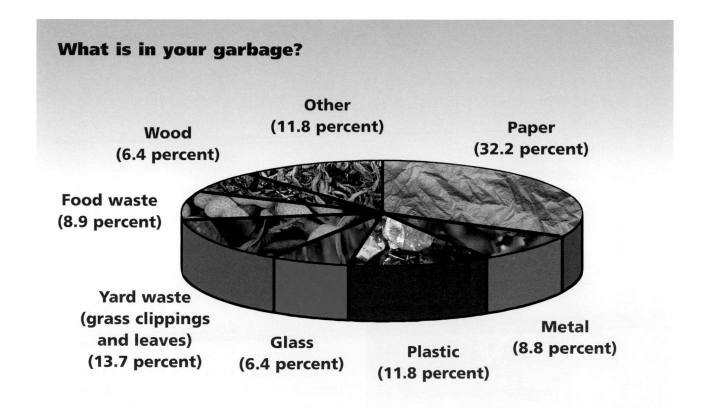

Other (11.8 percent)

Wood (6.4 percent)

Paper (32.2 percent)

Food waste (8.9 percent)

Yard waste (grass clippings and leaves) (13.7 percent)

Glass (6.4 percent)

Plastic (11.8 percent)

Metal (8.8 percent)

What types of waste are there?

Businesses and people create different kinds of waste. Some of it is dangerous and should never end up in a trash can. There are many different types of garbage, and they all need to be dealt with in different ways.

Municipal solid waste

Municipal solid waste is the proper name for regular garbage. This is everyday garbage, such as grass clippings or discarded food, debris from construction projects like old lumber or carpeting, and litter swept up on the street.

The amount of municipal solid waste has increased steadily since World War II. New methods of using plastics led to more **disposable** products and packaging. In addition, a strengthening economy in the United States allowed people to buy more items and keep things for less time before replacing them. The more people began to think of their belongings as disposable, the worse the trash problem became.

Hazardous waste

Hazardous means dangerous to humans, animals, or the environment, either immediately or in the future. As surprising as it may sound, hazardous materials are used every day in our homes. Examples of hazardous materials include gasoline, car batteries, bleach, and paint. When thrown away, all of these items can cause damage to people and the environment. These materials can make humans sick, release toxic fumes, or catch fire easily. Some kinds of **hazardous waste**, such as radioactive materials from nuclear power plants, will remain unsafe for thousands of years. Since these items can be dangerous, there are strict rules about the disposal of hazardous waste.

An estimated 136 million tons (123 million tonnes) of building-related construction and demolition debris is generated every year in the United States. Most of it ends up in city landfills.

What is liquid waste?

Sewage

Waste can be in liquid form as well as solid form. Liquid waste, which is usually called wastewater, can come from factories, households, and rainwater that is not absorbed into the ground. All wastewater eventually ends up in our rivers, lakes, or oceans.

First, though, wastewater must go through a cleaning process. In a city or suburban area, most wastewater is treated at a sewage treatment plant. In these plants, wastewater is treated to remove as much waste from it as possible. Once this is done, the treated wastewater is released.

In areas that do not have a central treatment plant, households install their own private treatment devices called septic tanks. Some communities, however, do not have the money or resources to keep water supplies clean. Untreated wastewater can then flow into rivers, lakes, and oceans. The wastewater will often contain **contaminants** such as gasoline, paint, pesticides, human waste from toilets, and trash. When untreated wastewater is released, it can cause severe damage to water supplies.

About 40 to 60 percent of solids are physically removed from wastewater in the initial treatment process. A secondary treatment biologically reduces organic materials that remain in the water.

Power plants contribute to liquid waste. Pollution from the plants causes acid rain, which negatively affects water quality.

How much garbage do we throw away?

In the 1890s, the majority of waste was ash. Homes were heated by wood and coal fires, which created ash. At the time, people rarely had garbage cans in their homes. Kitchen waste was fed to dogs and farm animals, thrown into the street or garden, or burned.

In the 1950s, the United States economy began to grow quickly. Natural resources were seen as limitless, especially petroleum for powering factories and making products like plastics. As the economy strengthened, people began to earn more money and buy more products, such as clothing, cars, and furniture. People worried less about throwing things away because it was easy and cheap to buy replacements. People did not think about recycling because no one worried about using up natural resources. Nor did they imagine that the space for storing trash would ever run out. Today, many people still do not stop to think about what they throw away.

BYTE-SIZED FACT
A family of four throws away about 80 to 150 pounds (36 to 68 kg) of garbage each week.

Individual Americans and American businesses throw out more than 1 million pounds (500,000 kg) of waste per person per year. This includes:

- **3.5 billion pounds (1.6 billion kg) of carpet,**

- **28 billion pounds (13 billion kg) of food,**

- **300 billion pounds (136 billion kg) of chemicals used in industries, and**

- **700 billion pounds (317 billion kg) of hazardous waste.**

Scientist

Do scientists really care about garbage?

As the problem of too much garbage grows each year, many scientists are dedicating their careers to finding other methods of solid waste disposal.

For a long time, garbage was not a problem. It was simply left on the curb and hauled away to a dump. This method worked well for a long time because most garbage was **biodegradable**, meaning it would disappear with time.

Over the past 50 years, new inventions have introduced materials that do not disappear as easily. The garbage that disappears with time is now a thing of the past. These new materials are sturdy and strong, built to stand the test of time. An aluminum can takes 200 to 500 years to break down. A Styrofoam cup will never break down.

Nonbiodegradable trash became a problem when populations began to grow.

People began running out of places to put their trash.

To fight this problem, scientists are trying to develop new ways to get rid of garbage. They are also trying to find new and better ways to recycle items, so people will not need to throw away as much as they currently do.

Scientists study how quickly garbage decays in landfills and conduct research to help create better systems of waste disposal.

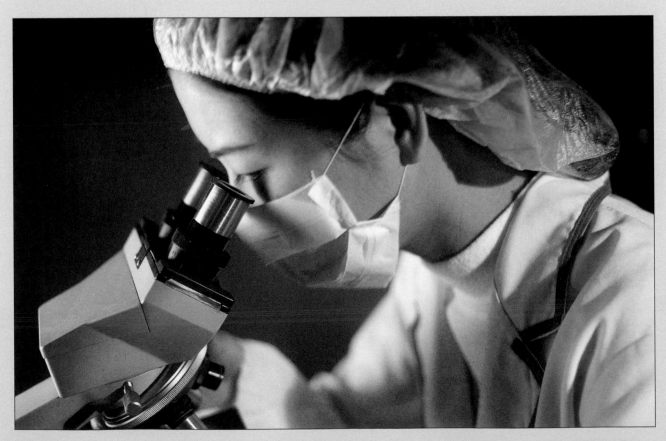

Where does the garbage go when we throw it away?

The United States is a large country with a huge population. The citizens create about 605,000 tons (549,000 tonnes) of solid trash per day. Fifty-seven percent of that trash goes into landfills, 16 percent is burned, and 27 percent is recycled.

Landfills

Garbage can end up in two different places. It can be put into a dump or a landfill.

A dump is a place where garbage is piled in the open air. Dumps cause many problems. They use up valuable land, they can harm the environment, they can attract rats, and they smell.

A landfill is a carefully designed structure that is built into the ground. It is placed away from important environmental areas, such as water sources.

Landfills have a clay or plastic liner in the bottom to help prevent **contamination** of **groundwater** and soil. They also have a cap or cover on top to keep pests, such as scavenging birds, animals, and insects, from getting into the trash. Caps also keep oxygen and moisture out. Trash is compacted, or squished, into spaces called cells. The trash is compacted so the landfill can hold more waste. Landfills are not designed to break down garbage, but rather to store as much waste as possible. Landfills must comply with strict federal and state regulations to ensure the environment does not become polluted.

BYTE-SIZED FACT

The number of landfills in the United States decreased from 8,000 in 1988 to 2,300 in 1999. However, newer landfills are much larger, so the amount of waste they can hold collectively remains the same. The number of landfills in the United States has decreased because state and local regulations are making it harder to construct new landfills.

How can waste be reduced?

Combustion

Burning is another way to reduce waste. The resulting ash is buried in a landfill. Burning can reduce the amount of waste sent to a landfill by 75 percent.

Unfortunately, burning can release toxic (poisonous) materials into the air. **Incinerators**, which are furnaces used to burn waste material, use technology to reduce toxic **emissions**. Burning waste at very high temperatures also reduces the amount of toxic materials released.

BYTE-SIZED FACT

In 1999, there were 102 incinerators in the United States, which were able to burn 96,000 tons (87,000 tonnes) of waste per day.

Recycling

Recycling prevents reusable material from ending up in a landfill or incinerator. People are becoming more aware of the importance of recycling. In 1999, 64 million tons (58 million tonnes) of waste were recycled. This is a major increase from the 34 million tons (31 million tonnes) of waste that were recycled in 1990.

Currently, more than half of all aluminum products are recycled. A recycled soup can may be back on store shelves in some other form within six weeks. About 38 percent of paper, such as newspaper, is recycled. About 20 percent of glass and about 5 percent of plastic are being recycled. Close to half of all recycled plastics are soda bottles. Glass and plastic are not recycled as much because these materials are expensive to process.

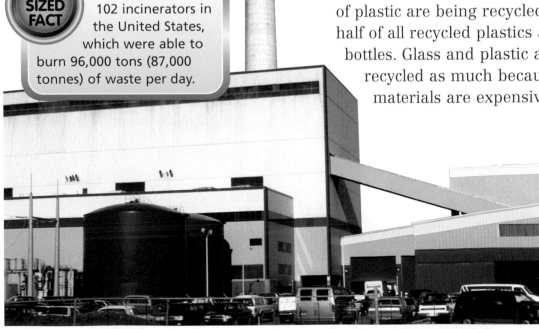

How is a landfill made?

A landfill is more complicated than just throwing garbage into a hole in the ground.

Before a landfill can be built, scientists must study the impact it will have on the surrounding environment. They look at the soil, bedrock, and flow of water in the area planned for the landfill. They also study possible effects on the wildlife in the area. The historical value of the area must be considered as well.

Once scientists decide that a landfill can be built on a site, it is necessary to obtain permits from the local, state, and federal governments.

The basic components of a landfill are the bottom liner and the drainage

Dump trucks can carry up to 25.5 tons (23 tonnes) of garbage to landfills in each load.

system. The liner keeps the trash separate from the groundwater, and the drainage system collects the water that falls on the landfill. There is also a system installed to collect the liquid formed by water dripping through the landfill. This liquid is collected to prevent water contamination. Another machine collects **methane** gas, which is formed during the breakdown of the trash. In some cases, methane gas is collected and used to generate electricity. A cover seals off the top of the landfill.

A working landfill must be open every day. Trash collectors and construction companies as well as individual citizens use landfills. When it enters a landfill, the vehicle containing the trash is weighed. The customer is charged a fee to use the landfill based on the weight of their garbage.

When a landfill is closed, a protective cover is built, and leaks and gas emissions are monitored. The cover structure includes a gas collecting and venting layer, a tightly sealed barrier layer, a drainage layer, and a top layer that is often covered in vegetation. Many landfills are turned into parks or golf courses when they close.

> The highest point in Ohio is "Mount Rumpke," which is actually a mountain of trash at the Rumpke sanitary landfill.
>
> **BYTE-SIZED FACT**

Does your school make too much trash?

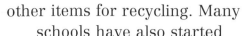

Every day in your classroom, you create waste. From leftover lunches and snacks to scrap paper and other school supplies, schools contribute to the problem of increasing garbage.

To prevent their trash from ending up in landfills and incinerators, many schools have recycling programs. Schools collect paper, beverage containers, and other items for recycling. Many schools have also started to cut down on materials used in classrooms. They encourage students and teachers to reuse other items when possible, such as printer ink cartridges (which can be refilled), rather than immediately throwing them away.

Much of the paper that ends up in classroom trash cans is recyclable.

Here is your challenge:

What kinds of trash does your class produce?

In your classroom, save the trash that is thrown away during an entire day. As a group with your teacher, go through the saved trash and separate it into three groups: trash that can be recycled, trash that can biodegrade, and anything else that must be thrown away.

Reusables and recyclables

Discuss some ways in which these materials can be reused or recycled. Plastic containers can be used many times; various types of paper can be recycled.

Biodegradables

Biodegradable materials will rot in a short period of time. Select a location on your schoolyard to bury some samples of biodegradable trash. Be sure no toxic materials are buried. Unearth the trash periodically to see what is happening. Record what you see. You can also bury paper, glass, or metal trash at the same time for comparison.

Nonbiodegradables

Nonbiodegradable materials will not decay and cannot be recycled. Could some reusable or recyclable materials have been substituted for disposable materials? Discuss what happens to trash in your community.

Misuse

"Waste not, want not."

With so many people creating so much garbage, there is bound to be a problem. Eventually there is no place left to put it.

All of our current methods of getting rid of garbage have problems. As the amount of waste increases, there will have to be changes in the way we deal with it in the future.

Can we just burn trash?

If there are large amounts of waste, and not enough room in landfills, why not burn the trash? It seems like the perfect solution. Unfortunately, burning garbage does not completely solve waste problems. In fact, burning creates some new problems.

Modern incinerators have powerful pollution-control technologies. They trap ash and harmful air pollution, and prevent it from getting into the environment. Unfortunately, none of these controls are completely effective. Some smoke and ash containing dangerous material can be released into the air.

When garbage is burned, about 40 percent of the waste remains in the form of ash. Though some ash is reused in products like cement, some ends up buried in a landfill.

The ash that results from burned garbage can be toxic. This means that it can be dangerous to humans and animals. Materials such as **dioxins** and **furans** are formed during the burning process. These materials are known to cause cancer. Toxic ash can

Burning garbage in a bonfire or an incinerator can be an effective way to reduce the amount of garbage. Still, it is not an ideal solution because of the toxic emissions that result.

only be buried in landfills built to contain hazardous materials. There is always a chance that these toxic materials might get into the water supply.

It is expensive to build and run incinerators. A modern incinerator can cost up to $600 million to build and another $300 million for pollution control.

Before modern incinerators existed, people would often burn their own trash. Today, some people still do this, especially in rural areas far away from dumps, landfills, or incinerators. This is a problem because there is no way to control the toxins that are released. According to the U.S. Environmental Protection Agency, backyard garbage burning, in fact, is now considered the primary source of dioxins in the air.

Because of the many problems with burning trash, incineration is not likely to be the cure for our garbage problems. Other methods will have to be explored.

What is the problem with landfills?

About 57 percent of garbage ends up in landfills. While this method of garbage disposal has worked well in the past, it has become less effective.

One of the main problems with landfills is that even the biodegradable garbage inside does not break down very well. This is because landfills have airtight and watertight linings and covers. These covers keep liquid from trash, known as **leachate**, from seeping into soil or groundwater. Unfortunately, these barriers also keep out oxygen and additional moisture needed for garbage to biodegrade.

Landfills end up storing waste, not biodegrading it. This means that landfills become full quickly, and new sites for landfills are constantly needed.

In addition, the liners at the bottom of landfills are not completely effective. Over time, they can develop cracks that allow leachate to seep through. Leachate could leak into groundwater and eventually contaminate drinking water supplies. Some of these toxins are known to cause health problems, including cancer.

There are strict rules prohibiting toxic waste from being disposed of in regular city landfills. Even so, these landfills may still contain hazardous materials. Sometimes, toxic waste is illegally dumped in them. Other times, garbage can chemically react to produce toxins when different types are mixed together.

BYTE-SIZED FACT

Seventy percent of the garbage that ends up in landfills could have been recycled or reused. Landfills have very little oxygen and moisture. Because of this, the garbage breaks down slowly. One old landfill was excavated and a 40-year-old newspaper was found. The newspaper had barely broken down, and the print remained easy to read.

Sometimes the systems designed to keep landfills airtight and watertight can break down, which causes additional problems. Landfills have a drainage system that collects rainwater and stops it from seeping into the landfill and possibly leaking into the groundwater. Mud may clog the drainage systems, or chemicals may weaken the pipes. If problems like these prevent the system from working properly, rainwater may enter and leave the landfill.

Over time, a landfill's cap may crack or buckle, allowing air and moisture to enter the landfill. Sunlight, wind, and rain can weaken the cap in a process called **erosion**. Roots from nearby trees and shrubs can also push up against the cover, causing it to buckle or crack. Even the trash underneath may shift and push up against the cover, causing it to buckle.

Here is your challenge:

Make a miniature landfill and an open dump. First, ask an adult for permission to perform this activity.

You will need:

- Two large containers, such as glass jars or milk cartons
- Several pieces of fruit, such as a slice of tomato or an apple core
- Two small pieces of plastic such as a plastic fork or part of a broken toy
- Several small pieces of newspaper
- Soil

The first container will be the landfill. Place some soil in the bottom of it. On top of the soil, place half of the fruit pieces and one of the plastic forks. Take one of the small pieces of newspaper and crumple it into a tight ball. Take another

and rip it into many small pieces. Place all of this on top of the soil. Add more soil on top of these items, covering them completely.

The second container will be the open dump. Fill the second container almost full of soil. Dig a hole in the soil and place fruit, a plastic fork, and a crumpled and torn newspaper inside the hole. Do not cover these items up.

Put the containers in a warm place and keep the soil damp. After one week, check to see what has happened to the fruit, the paper, and the plastic. Are there odor differences between the two containers? What would happen if a strong wind blew across your second container, the open dump?

Paper or plastic?

At the grocery store, people are often asked if they want paper or plastic bags to hold their groceries. Some people choose paper. Others choose plastic. These people may believe one type of bag is better for the environment or produces less waste. Paper and plastic both have advantages and disadvantages, but it is difficult to determine if one is actually better than the other.

Plastic was once thought of as the "wonder material." Made from petroleum byproducts, it is light, lasts a very long time, and can be used in many ways.

Americans use about 14 billion pounds (5 billion kg) of plastic each year, compared to 171 billion pounds (77.5 billion kg) of paper.

Plastic makes up about 8 percent of the waste in landfills. The problem with plastic is that it is not really biodegradable. This means that it does not break down and disappear over time.

Many people choose paper over plastic bags at the grocery store because paper bags are easier to recycle. Paper is more commonly accepted in recycling programs.

Plastics are made from petroleum byproducts. There are seven different types of plastics used in packaging. Most states require plastic containers to have identification codes so they can be easily identified and separated.

Plastic can be recycled, but only through a complicated process. There are many different types of plastics that must be sorted before they can be recycled. In addition, plastic can only be recycled once or twice because the quality of the plastic decreases each time.

Paper makes up about 40 to 50 percent of waste in landfills. However, over time, paper should break down and disappear. Paper is easily recycled and can be reused many times before the fibers in the paper become unusable.

These advantages may make paper seem like a better choice than plastic, but there are other factors to consider. The lack of oxygen and moisture in landfills means nothing really biodegrades—not even paper.

Plastic takes up very little space in landfills. Plastic is very easy to compact, meaning that it can be squished so it takes up less space. Although a lot of plastic is produced, the space it takes up in landfills is decreasing. This is because plastic is becoming less bulky. Scientists are also working on making a biodegradable plastic.

Paper is easy to recycle because it is made from pulp. When paper is recycled it is put in a machine that works like a giant blender. The ink separates from the paper fibers and floats to the surface. Then the clean fibers are mixed with new wood fibers to be made into paper again.

Paper and plastic are used in many kinds of packaging materials. After packaging materials have been used one time, they are often thrown away. Regardless of whether you use paper or plastic, it is important to begin recycling these items. Doing so will help to reduce the amount of waste in landfills.

Your family could also bring cloth bags to the store to carry groceries home. In this way, you will not add to the excess garbage problem at all.

BYTE-SIZED FACT Americans use four million plastic bottles every hour. Only one out of four bottles is recycled after use.

What's the problem with packaging?

When you buy an item at the store, it often comes wrapped up in something, usually plastic, paper, cardboard, or glass.

When you open the package and take out the item, what happens to the packaging? Does the packaging get used, recycled, or thrown away?

In the United States, packaging materials make up one-third of all waste. Packaging materials include not only fast-food boxes, plastic bags, and cans but also wooden pallets, cardboard cartons, plastic wrap, and crates, all of which protect the products before they get to store shelves.

Products use packaging for a number of reasons. It helps to reduce theft and tampering, prevents products from breaking, and keeps food items fresh. It can make products easier to handle by adding features like handles or spouts. Finally, packaging provides a surface for written information about the product.

Packaging has important uses. Still, the amount of packaging being used today is a problem. Some manufacturers have reduced the amount of packaging they use for their products. They are using thinner, lighter, and fewer plastics, metals, and paper. Some have also started to use biodegradable packing peanuts made from cornstarch rather than polystyrene plastic.

Doing this cuts down on the amount of garbage, saves money on materials, and reduces shipping costs. People can also help reduce the amount of packaging waste by buying products that have little or no packaging.

About 200 million cubic feet (61 million cu m) of polystyrene packaging material is used every year in the United States. Although some companies and individuals try to reuse the packing material, most is disposed of in landfills.

A single piece of cardboard can be recycled eight times. Every ton (0.9 tonnes) of paper that is recycled saves seventeen trees.

BYTE-SIZED FACT

In 1970, a half-gallon (2 l) plastic soda bottle weighed 2.1 ounces (60 g). Today that same bottle weighs only 1.7 ounces (48 g). It is also more compact.

Are we recycling enough?

People are now recycling less than they did in the 1990s. For the first time in twenty years, Americans are throwing away more aluminum cans than they recycle.

There are several possible reasons for this decline in recycling. Many cities have curbside pickup of recycling materials. Programs like this cost money, and if a city is having financial problems, the program may be stopped. If this happens, less waste is recycled because individuals are less likely to drop off recyclables at recycling centers.

BYTE-SIZED FACT In 2001, 49 percent of the aluminum cans sold in the United States were recycled. In 1991, 60 percent were recycled.

The price of aluminum scrap metal has also dropped because of decreased demand for aluminum products, which is a result of a slowdown in the global economy. Recycling aluminum cans provides less money than it once did.

In addition, the cost of making products from recycled materials is higher than the cost of making new products. Before recyclable material can be reused, it must be sorted, cleaned, and processed. Companies that process recyclables must pay people to do this extra work. They then charge higher prices to other companies that want to buy recycled materials for use in their own products. The result is that many companies are not willing to use recycled materials at all.

Despite the costs, recycling has many benefits. It takes a large amount of energy to make aluminum. Producing a soda can from recycled aluminum uses 96 percent less energy and produces 95 percent less air pollution and 97 percent less water pollution than manufacturing a new can.

The long-term cost savings and advantages make recycling good for the environment and for people. However, until the price of recycled materials goes down, or laws are passed requiring companies to use these materials, a major improvement in the amount of recycling performed in the United States is unlikely.

Is there waste in the air?

Air pollution is a major concern. There are many sources of air pollution, including factories and smoke from incinerators.

Vehicles such as cars, buses, and trucks also cause air pollution. More than 200 million vehicles are registered in the United States.

Emissions from vehicles, which are materials released into the air when car engines burn fuel, not only affect air quality but also add to the **greenhouse effect**, also known as global warming. Vehicles can also release toxic materials into the air, some of which are known to cause cancer.

Scientists and engineers have been designing vehicles that use different sources of fuel. These new vehicles run on electricity and natural gas, resulting in much lower emissions. Some of these vehicles are on the market now.

Other companies are producing cleaner gas, which also results in lower emissions. In addition, some states are enforcing tougher emission standards, which means that people are only allowed to drive cars that produce low emissions.

BYTE-SIZED FACT

It would take twenty new cars to generate the same amount of air pollution as one car from the mid-1960s. Unfortunately, the distance people drive every day has increased since the 1960s, so overall air pollution has become worse instead of better.

What are greenhouse gases?

Component	Effect
Carbon monoxide	Poisonous gas
Particulate (soot)	Contains chemicals known to cause cancer
Lead	Poisonous
Greenhouse gases, including:	
• Carbon dioxide	Major cause of global warming
• Nitrogen oxides	Contribute to acid rain and smog; cause breathing problems
• Hydrocarbons	Contribute to smog; have an unpleasant smell
• Sulfur oxides	Contribute to acid rain

Is land being wasted?

As the population of the United States grows, so does the size of cities and towns. This is a phenomenon known as urban sprawl. Between 1992 and 1997, 16 million acres (6.5 million hectares) of land in the United States were converted into houses, malls, and parking lots. This rate of development is two times higher than it was ten years ago.

One of the problems with increasing development is that it seems to be happening at a faster rate than the population is growing. For example, in New York between 1970 and 1990, the population grew by only about 5 percent, but land use increased by 61 percent. At this rate, there will not be any land left.

Increased development also creates a number of other problems. These include increased waste production, traffic congestion, air pollution, and energy use.

One concern about land development is the loss of farmland and **habitat** for native animals. Long-term habitat loss is one of the main reasons that animal species are becoming **extinct**. Without a place to live, an animal cannot survive.

BYTE-SIZED FACT

In the United States, 30 acres (12 hectares) of forest and farmland is lost to development each minute.

Leachate in groundwater

Liquid formed from waste in landfills is called leachate. Groundwater contamination from leachate is a major concern.

The U.S. Environmental Protection Agency (EPA) estimates that 75 percent of landfills are polluting groundwater. Groundwater is the water that lies beneath the **water table**. This water flows slowly but eventually emerges from underground into lakes, rivers, streams, or the ocean.

If leachate enters groundwater, it can cause a number of problems. It may even make the water unusable.

Leachate in groundwater can affect the taste and odor of the water, or it can reduce the amount of oxygen, which would affect fish and water plants. If the leachate is toxic, the water could make people and animals sick.

Municipal landfills are not supposed to have hazardous materials in them. Toxic substances may form in leachate through reactions with other substances in the garbage. The resulting toxic

materials could cause cancer or birth defects.

Many of these materials have not yet been thoroughly studied by scientists. This means that the possible effects of these materials on groundwater are also unknown.

Leachate enters groundwater from waste in landfills. The contaminated groundwater can enter water supply wells of homes, or enter lakes, rivers, and streams.

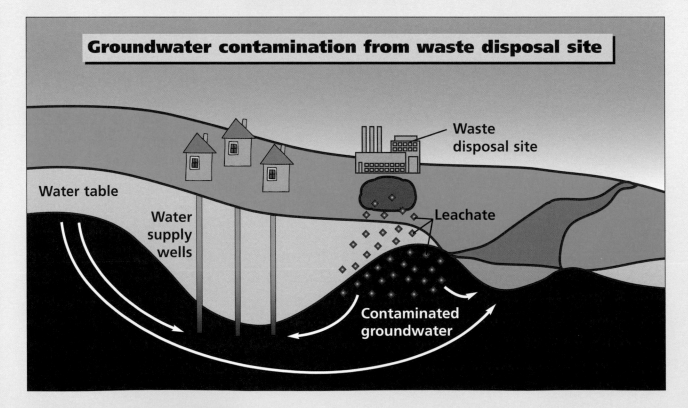

Groundwater contamination from waste disposal site

Water table

Water supply wells

Waste disposal site

Leachate

Contaminated groundwater

A landfill does not only produce leachate while it is in operation. Studies have found that landfills that have been closed for decades are still producing leachate.

If groundwater is contaminated by leachate, it has to be treated in a water treatment plant before it is considered safe. This treatment can be expensive and may not guarantee that all the leachate has been removed.

In the United States, the Environmental Protection Agency sets standards for drinking water under the Safe Drinking Water Act. However, many Americans have tap water that fails to meet these standards.

Here is your challenge:

When water sinks through the ground, the layers of rocks, sand, and dirt act as a filter to help purify it. But this process cannot remove every kind of contaminant. In this challenge you will observe the types of contaminants that can be filtered out using a basic filtering system. Take two Styrofoam cups and poke ten small holes in the bottom with a sharpened pencil. Layer both cups with cotton, gravel, sand, and bits of grass.

Add a spoonful of dirt into 1 cup of tap water. After mixing in the dirt, pour 3/4-cup of water into one of the Styrofoam cups, setting the remaining 1/4-cup of dirty water aside. Hold the cup over a glass to catch the water that comes through the holes. Does the water that comes out look different than the dirty water that you set aside?

Now take another cup of water and add a spoonful of dirt as well as a few drops of blue food coloring. The food coloring represents chemicals dissolved in the water. After mixing the dirt into the water thoroughly, filter 3/4-cup of it through the second Styrofoam cup. Compare the water that comes out with the 1/4-cup of water that was not filtered. Did the filtering process remove any of the food coloring?
Note: Do not drink any of the water!

Reuse

"Use it up,
wear it out,
make it do,
or do without."

The three "Rs"—reduce, reuse, and recycle—are as important as ever. The amount of trash thrown away needs to be reduced. Containers and products should be reused whenever possible. Products also need to be recycled as often as possible, and people should make an effort to buy products with recycled content.

For example, McDonald's recently identified 200 items in their restaurants that can be made from recycled materials. These items include bags and cartons, tables and chairs, booster seats for children, serving trays, and building materials. By 1999 McDonald's had spent $3 billion on recycled products and materials to build, remodel, and equip its restaurants.

What does biodegradable mean?

When a material is biodegradable, it means that living things can break it down. Under the right conditions, material can be broken down into simple **compounds**, such as carbon dioxide and water. The process of decay releases these compounds back into the environment so that they can be used again.

Decay may seem a little unappealing, and people often try to stop it from happening. Putting grass clippings into a plastic bag and sending it to a landfill, rather than **composting** it, is an example of this attitude toward waste. If nothing were recycled, the nutrients and resources in the world would be used up entirely.

Many things are needed for a material to biodegrade. Bacteria and other simple organisms in soil eat and digest biodegradable material. Insects and worms do the same thing, breaking down materials. Oxygen and moisture are also usually needed, as well as the right temperature.

Different materials break down at different rates. How long a material takes to **decompose** depends on its content.

Leaving cars to decompose is an environmental problem. Many car parts, such as plastic headlight covers, are not biodegradable.

BYTE-SIZED FACT

A piece of food can take only one week or two to biodegrade outside of a landfill, while a tin can may take 100 to 500 years.

What are the three Rs?

Reduce

Reducing waste means that less garbage will be thrown away and landfills will take longer to fill up. There are many ways to cut down on waste. When shopping, you can buy products that are made to last or are reusable. Also, choosing products with less packaging means that less trash will be thrown away.

The three arrows in the recycling symbol stand for the three steps in the process of recycling: separating trash from recyclable materials, manufacturing new products from recycled materials, and buying products made with recycled materials.

WE RECYCLE

Recycle

Recycling turns potential waste into new products. Recycling not only saves items from ending up in a landfill or incinerator, it also helps the environment by preventing new resources from being used to make the same products. For example, recycling paper saves trees from being cut down. Also, recycling tin cans means that new metals will not have to be mined. This saves energy and reduces the pollution caused by mining activities.

Reuse

Similar to reducing waste, reusing products means that less waste will end up in a landfill. If it is not possible to reuse an item, it does not have to be thrown away. Instead, the item can be given away or sold to allow someone else to use it. Also, if something is broken, it may be possible to fix it rather than throwing it away.

Tires can be reused as playground equipment, planters, and as an ingredient in asphalt.

How can we reduce, reuse, and recycle?

There are easy ways to reduce, reuse, and recycle.

- Use cloth napkins or towels instead of paper
- Refill, reuse, or recycle bottles
- Donate things that you no longer use to charities
- Use refillable pens and pencils
- Use empty jars to hold items such as leftover food
- Use rechargeable batteries
- Use cloth bags at the grocery store rather than paper or plastic
- Use grass clippings to make compost rather than throwing them away

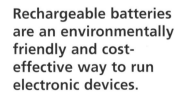

Rechargeable batteries are an environmentally friendly and cost-effective way to run electronic devices.

What is composting?

Composting is another form of recycling. It is also another way to reduce the amount of waste going into landfills. Composting is the controlled decomposition and decay of organic matter. Organic matter includes food waste, such as fruit and vegetable peels, leftovers, and eggshells. It also includes yard waste, such as grass clippings, leaves, and small weeds. This organic mixture decomposes into a soil-like material. Composting is nature's way of recycling.

Composting keeps organic waste out of landfills, where it would never break down. Composting ensures that these materials decompose and become useful to the environment.

Compost is used in flower and vegetable gardens and landscaping. It can be added to soil as fertilizer to make flowers and vegetables grow well. Compost also reduces the need for chemical fertilizers and pesticides. Fertilizers and pesticides can be harmful to the environment, causing toxic materials to seep into the ground and even the water supply.

Composting has been known to prevent disease in plants, increase helpful soil organisms, such as worms, and protect soil from being washed away by rain or blown away by wind.

Composting in schools is becoming popular. With composting, students can see food scraps change into something that is good for the soil.

BYTE-SIZED FACT
More than 67 percent of waste produced in the United States (including paper) is compostable material. Anything that was once a plant can be composted (plus eggshells).

Here is your challenge:

Make your own composter

Composting is nature's way of recycling. Decay and decomposition happen no matter what you do. Since there is so much waste, composting is a good way to help the environment.

By making your own composter, you will learn about the process of decomposition, cut down on the garbage you throw away, and help plants in your garden grow.

For kitchen compost, you will need to collect some or all of the following ingredients: vegetable peels and seeds, fruit peels and seeds, coffee grounds, eggshells, nutshells, and any other vegetable or fruit scraps. Do not add meat scraps, bones, dairy products, oil, or fat, because these things may attract animals or other pests.

Once done, your compost should look like dark crumbly soil mixed with small pieces of organic material. It should have a sweet, earthy smell. Feed the compost to plants by mixing it with soil.

Compost instructions:

1. Choose a container such as a chicken wire box or a wooden box. It should be about 4 cubic feet (0.1 cu m) in size.
2. Place kitchen wastes into the composting container. Have an adult help you to chop or shred the waste if you want it to compost faster. Add kitchen waste and other organic material whenever you have some.
3. Spread soil over the top of the compost pile. This layer contains the **microorganisms** needed to make the compost. It also keeps the surface moist.
4. Add water or sawdust to make the pile wetter or drier. It should be damp to the touch.
5. Allow the compost pile to "bake" in a sunny area. It should heat up quickly.
6. Stir the pile with a shovel occasionally to speed up the process of decay. As composting occurs, the pile should begin to settle.
7. If you mix and turn it every week, your compost will be ready for use in one month or two. If not, it could take up to twelve months.

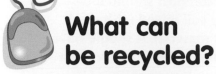

What can be recycled?

Many everyday items can be recycled. If an effort were made to recycle all of these items, much less waste would end up in landfills or incinerators. Recycling also saves energy and resources, and reduces air and water pollution.

Aluminum

Manufacturing a can from recycled aluminum reduces air and water pollution by 94 percent compared to manufacturing a can from raw materials. Recycling one aluminum can saves enough energy to run a television for three hours. Enough aluminum is thrown away to rebuild the entire U.S. commercial airline fleet four times a year.

Glass

Manufacturing a glass bottle from recycled glass reduces air pollution by 20 percent and water pollution by 50 percent compared to manufacturing glass from raw materials. By recycling one glass jar, enough energy is saved to light a 100-watt bulb for four hours. Glass can be recycled many times.

Paper

Manufacturing paper products from recycled paper reduces air and water pollution 55 percent compared to manufacturing paper from new wood. Currently, enough paper is thrown away every year to build a 12-foot (4 m) wall from New York to California.

Plastic

The United States uses 14 billion pounds (6.4 billion kg) of plastics each year, but only about 5 percent is recycled. The recycled plastics are used to make fibers, containers, bottles, pipes, lawn and garden products, and car parts.

Steel

Each year, recycling steel saves enough energy to supply electricity to 18 million homes for one year. It also reduces the mining of resources, such as iron ore, coal, and limestone. Currently, the amount of iron and steel thrown away could be used to supply the nation's automakers continually.

Is a pay-as-you-throw (PAYT) program a good idea?

Many states are starting programs where residents pay for the amount of trash they throw away. It is hoped this will reduce the amount of garbage, as well as encourage recycling.

In the past, people paid a fixed amount for garbage collection. The amount was the same no matter how much—or how little—garbage they threw out. The PAYT program is similar to paying for electricity or water. The amount you pay depends on the amount of garbage you throw out. The less you throw out, the less you pay.

Some people do not believe the PAYT program is as good as it claims. They fear that it will result in illegal dumping of waste by people not wanting to pay. Many critics believe that it is unfair to poorer families.

"It makes trash removal like a utility. You pay for what you use. Recycling rates double, sometimes triple, and that's in town after town." **Planner with state planning office in Augusta, Georgia**

"The cost savings would be 'in the bag.' If you throw away a little, you pay a little; if you throw away a lot, you pay a lot." **New Hampshire Recycling Committee Vice Chairman**

"Taxpayers won't buy into the plan, and it will cause more problems, such as illegal dumping." **New Hampshire Selectmen Chairman**

"There's not a great deal of public support for the pay-as-you-throw program. It is too much too soon." **Town Manager, Pittsfield, Maine**

What do you think about a PAYT program?
Is it a good idea?
Would you want to be a part of this program?

Wet landfills

Researchers are working on the problem of disappearing landfill space. With increasing garbage going into landfills, they are becoming full at a faster rate. Once landfills become full, new areas have to be found to build more landfills.

One of the reasons landfills are becoming so full so fast is that very little decomposition takes place inside them.

A scientific study found that if a landfill is kept moist, the trash inside will decompose much faster. On average, a landfill will take about 100 years to decompose. A moist landfill can decompose in just five to ten years. If a landfill is kept moist enough, bacteria will begin decomposition at a faster rate.

Leachates are a problem with many sanitary, or sealed, landfills. In wet landfills, the leachates are collected and recirculated back into the garbage.

With this process, landfills would become more like treatment facilities, rather than storage facilities. A wet landfill would continually decompose old trash, creating room for new trash to be added. This would cut down on the land needed for landfills.

In a traditional landfill, waste is spread in thin layers and compacted by bulldozers. When a 10 foot (3 m) layer of waste has been laid down, it is covered by a layer of clean earth.

Environmental engineer

If the environment interests you, then you should consider a career as an environmental engineer.

An environmental engineer designs and maintains pollution control techniques, designs landfills, and develops systems to reverse damage done to the environment. An environmental engineer's work may involve solid waste disposal, water and air pollution control, or controlling hazardous wastes.

In this job, you might work with people from all levels of government, as well as community groups and other scientists and engineers.

Environmental engineers usually have a degree in engineering from a university or college. Working as a volunteer in your city's environmental office would be a great way to see if this type of career is for you.

Environmental engineering is a rewarding career that helps both people and the environment.

Science Survey

Everybody creates garbage. Many people also recycle, reuse, and reduce their waste. Does your family recycle its garbage? Take this survey home to learn about your family's recycling habits.

What are your answers?

1. Which of the following items go into your garbage: cans, glass bottles, paper, Styrofoam, newspapers, grocery bags, batteries, clothing, disposable diapers?
2. Which of these items are recyclable?
3. Does your town or city have a place to recycle any of these items?
4. Where does your garbage go when it leaves your house?
5. How does reusing things help the environment?

Survey Results

Most of the items listed in question 1 are recyclable. When people throw away garbage, it usually ends up in a landfill. Landfill space is becoming scarce. Every time people throw something away, they also throw away the energy, money, raw materials, and water it took to make it. Recycling saves these items from ending up in a landfill, and allows materials in them to be reused.

Here is your challenge:

Collect a variety of household items that are thrown in the garbage. Try to include things that could be used again, such as grocery bags, aluminum foil, and plastic containers. Also include items that could be recycled, such as newspapers or glass jars.

Try to think of new uses for these items. Also think of ways to reduce the amount of reusable garbage you throw away.

These websites might help:

Make-Stuff.com
www.make-stuff.com/recycling/index.html

The Imagination Factory
www.kid-at-art.com

South Central Iowa Solid Waste Agency
www.sciswa.org/crafts.html

Fast Facts

1. The United States has 6 percent of the world's population and creates 50 percent of the world's garbage.

2. Every day, U.S. businesses use enough paper to circle Earth twenty times.

3. About 220 tons (200 tonnes) of computers and other electronic waste are dumped in landfills and incinerators every year in the United States.

4. Experts predict that most states will reach their landfill capacity in the next ten years.

5. Glass bottles will last for up to one million years if not recycled.

6. Americans receive about 52 billion pieces of advertising in their mailboxes every year.

7. In the 1900s, pigs were used to get rid of garbage in several cities. One expert reported that 75 pigs could eat 1 ton (0.9 tonnes) of garbage per day.

8. The first aluminum recycling plant opened in Chicago in 1904.

9. In 1690, paper was made from recycled fibers at a mill near Philadelphia.

10. If all Americans recycled just their Sunday paper, it would save an entire forest of 500,000 trees each week.

11. When 1 ton (0.9 tonnes) of paper is recycled, seventeen trees are saved.

12. Plastic lumber, made of recycled plastic, is being developed. It is currently used to build decks, park benches, and flower boxes. It is more durable than wood. Plastic lumber will help reduce the use of wood products in construction.

13. Recycling 1 ton (0.9 tonnes) of glass saves the equivalent in energy of 10 gallons (38 l) of oil.

14. An average family of four will throw away 10 to 15 pounds (4.5 to 6.8 kg) of food and about 10 pounds (4.5 kg) of paper in one week.

15. Forty-two percent of all paper, 40 percent of all plastic soft drink bottles, 55 percent of all aluminum drink cans, 57 percent of all steel packaging, and 52 percent of all major appliances are recycled.

16. Fourteen billion mail order catalogs are thrown away each year in the United States.

17. Not only does smoking cause lung cancer but it is also bad for the environment. Cigarette butts will last for one to five years before they decompose.

18. Nearly one-third of the garbage people throw away consists of product packaging materials.

19. Curbside recycling programs and drop-off recycling centers have prevented 28 percent of solid waste from being sent to U.S. landfills.

20. By 2005, at least 500 million cell phones will be ready for disposal in the United States. This means that 65,000 tons (58,968 tonnes) of trash is headed for landfills.

Young Scientists@Work

Test your knowledge of waste with these questions and activities. You can probably answer the questions using this book, your own experiences, and your common sense.

FACT:

Many items that are thrown away are actually recyclable.

TEST:

Which of the following items are recyclable?

Glass bottles, plastic containers, newspapers, tin cans, disposable diapers, leftover food, grass clippings, metal.

Answers:
Glass, plastics, newspapers, tin cans, and metal can all be recycled. Disposable diapers are not commonly recyclable. While leftover food and grass clippings cannot be recycled, they can be composted and added to soil.

Three Recycling Methods

FACT:
Different types of garbage should be dealt with in different ways.

TEST:
Look at the three photos of different types of garbage. Then, look at the three recycling methods of getting rid of garbage. Match each type of garbage to the best method of disposal.

1. Recycling center

2. Compost

3. Hazardous waste landfill

Answers:
1. Newspaper, glass bottles, tin cans—go to a recycling center.
2. Grass clippings and leftover food—make into compost.
3. Hazardous materials (bleach, paint, etc.)—hazardous waste landfill.

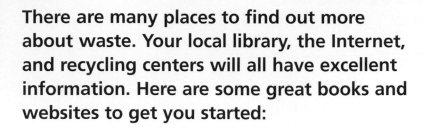

Research on Your Own

There are many places to find out more about waste. Your local library, the Internet, and recycling centers will all have excellent information. Here are some great books and websites to get you started:

Great Books

Parker, Steve. *Waste, Recycling and Re-use.* Chicago: Raintree, 1998.

Paulson, Rachael. *Sir Johnny's Recycling Adventure.* Sparta, N.J.: Crestmont Publishing, 1999.

Smith, Heather. *Earth-Friendly Crafts for Kids: 50 Awesome Things to Make with Recycled Stuff.* Asheville, N.C.: Lark Books, 2002.

Great Websites

U.S. Environmental Protection Agency Garbage and Recycling Kids' Pages
http://www.epa.gov/kids/garbage.htm

Kids Recycle!
http://www.kidsrecycle.org

Massachusetts Institute of Technology's Center for Environmental Health Sciences Kids' Pages
http://web.mit.edu/civenv/K12Edu

Glossary

biodegradable: able to be broken down by microorganisms into simpler forms

composting: breaking down organic materials, such as yard, garden, and kitchen wastes, to produce a rich, soil-like mixture

compounds: a whole formed by a union of two or more elements or parts (such as chemicals)

contaminants: substances that pollute another substance

contamination: the act or process of polluting one substance with another

decompose: to rot, break down, or decay

dioxins: toxic substances formed when materials are burned

disposable: meant to be thrown away after a single use or just a few uses

emissions: substances that are released into the air

environment: the surroundings of an organism that affect its development and survival

erosion: the wearing away of a surface by any natural process, such as water and wind

extinct: no longer alive anywhere

furans: toxic, flammable liquids

greenhouse effect: warming that results when solar radiation is trapped by the atmosphere

groundwater: water beneath the earth's surface between soil and deep layers of rock. This water supplies springs and wells, and may be used as drinking water.

habitat: the living area of a plant or animal

hazardous waste: a substance that is potentially damaging to the environment and harmful to humans and other living organisms

incinerator: furnace or other device used for burning waste

landfill: a system of garbage disposal in which waste is buried between layers of earth

leachate: water that leaks through a dump or landfill, picking up pollutants along the way

methane: a colorless, odorless, flammable gas

microorganisms: tiny living things that can only be seen through a microscope

recyclable: able to be used again

water table: the level in an area below which the ground is soaked with water

Index